100 Shiny Pennies

Written by Marelle Brewer
Illustrated by Tommy Norton

ISBN 978-0-9978127-1-8

For information regarding permission or to obtain
additional copies, email goshinethosepennies@gmail.com.

10 9 8 7 6 5 4

Profound gratitude to ALL of the individuals who have helped us "shine our pennies". You know who you are.

-M.B.

With all my heart I dedicate my art to those with special needs, their families, and my angel mother. I thank God every day for the talents He's given me.

-T.N.

PK had large blue eyes that often peeked over his little round glasses...

and a smile that made other people happy.

Even though he was smaller than other children his age, PK could do many things:

Race toy cars, play soccer and – from a VERY young age – build anything out of pretty much anything else!

His family never knew what amazing invention PK would dream up next!

As he grew, PK realized he was different from other children.

His mother did not know how to explain to him that three very large words described his three very real challenges, until...

one special day, when an idea came quietly into his mother's mind and heart.

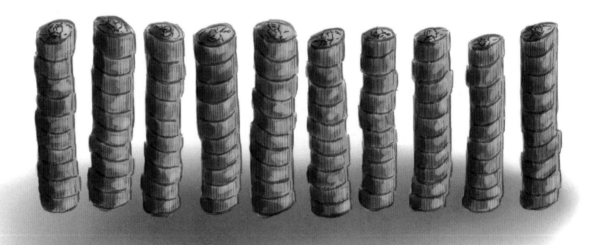

She asked PK to picture 100 pennies.
"Ten rows of ten pennies, right?"

"Yes", said PK.

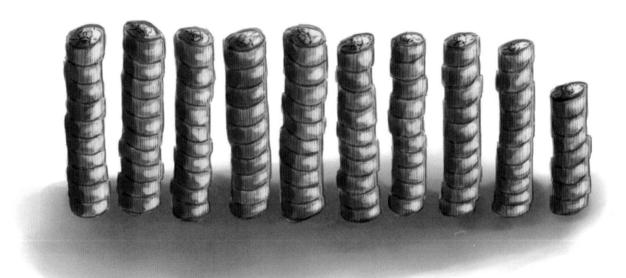

"Well," she said, "I believe if you were made of 100 pennies, then 97 of your pennies would be shiny."

He understood, so far, what she meant.

Then she said,
"If I take 97 away from 100, what do I have left?"

PK thought for a moment and replied,
"Three."

"That is correct," said his mother.

"I believe if you were made of 100 pennies, then 97 would be the shiny pennies and represent the many things you can do well, while only three of your pennies need help becoming shinier."

She further explained that the three less-shiny pennies were like the three sets of large words PK could not understand about himself and made him seem different from other children.

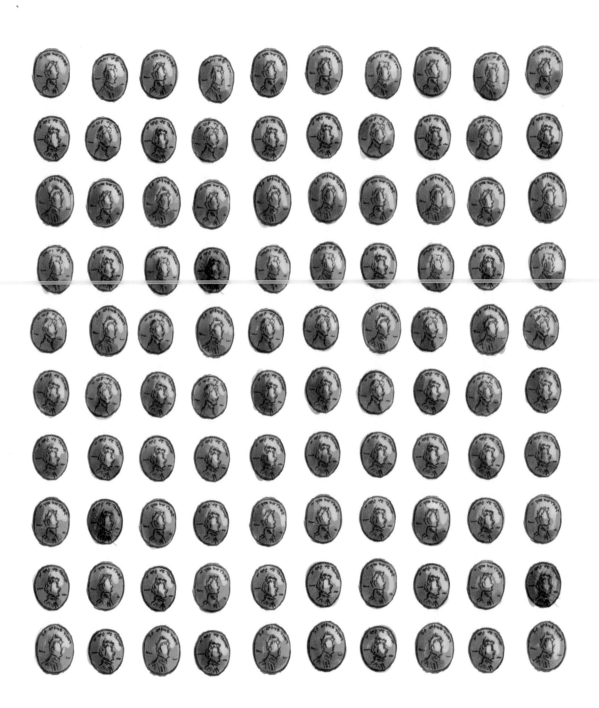

"You are very bright like the 97 shiny pennies and can do many great things," PK's mother said.

"We will just keep shining those three other pennies. There is SO much to learn, gain and share as we do this, even if it is hard at times. There is so much more to you than your less-shiny pennies."

She paused and added,

"Everyone has shiny and less-shiny pennies. We all have things we can do well, like the shiny pennies, and things that are hard for us to do, like the less-shiny pennies."

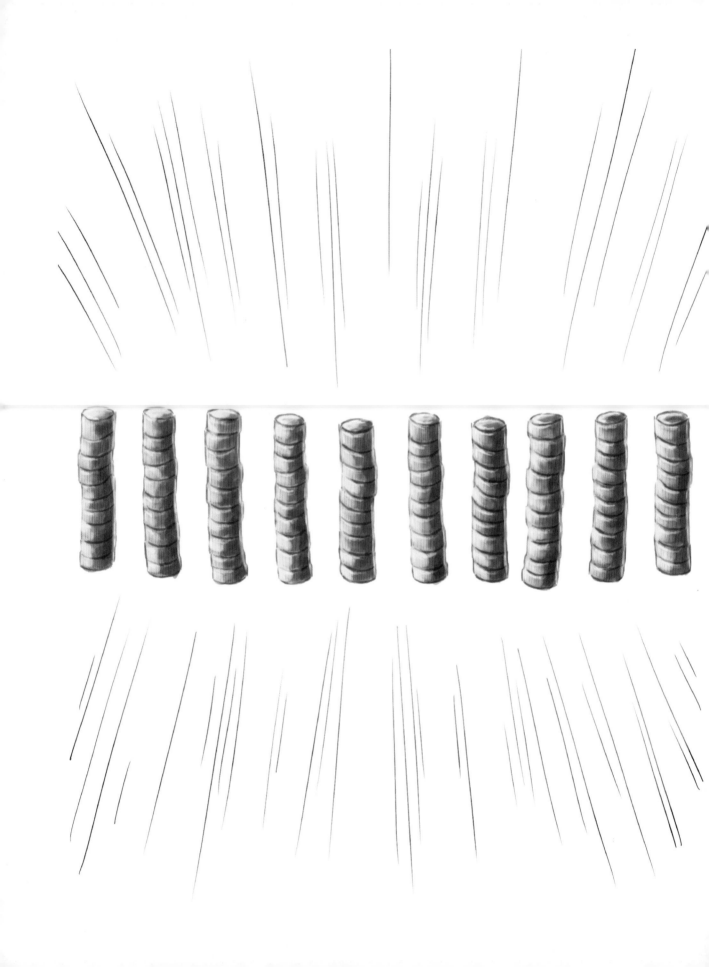

PK was silent for several seconds and then said very gently,

"Momma, Jesus is the only one with ALL 100 shiny pennies, right?"

This touched his mother's heart.

"Yes," she answered softly.

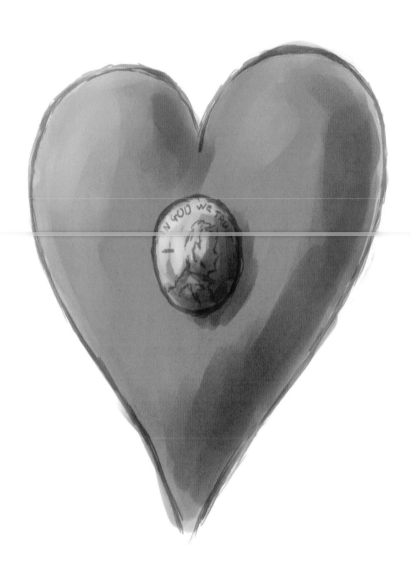

"Momma?"

"Yes, PK?"

"You are MY shiny penny."

"Thank you, PK," she answered as happy tears welled up in her eyes and fell gently onto her cheeks.

She was grateful for those tender moments with her son.

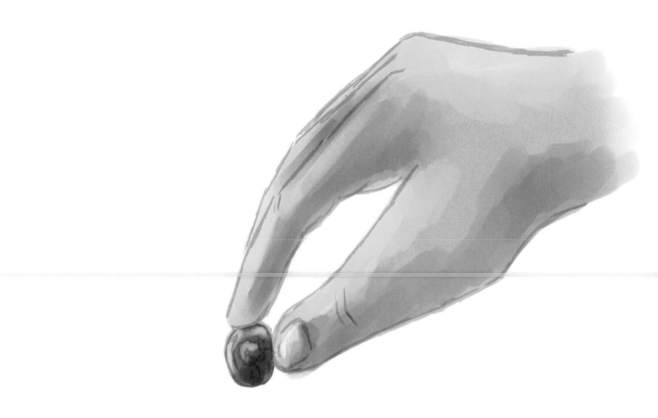

Since that special day, every time PK begins a new school year or faces another challenge, his mother carefully tucks the shiniest penny she can find into his hand and whispers in his ear, "Go shine those pennies!"

PK always looks up and smiles.

"Thanks Mom," he says, and off he bravely goes to keep shining his pennies.

PK knows he is not alone shining his pennies. Jesus and others help him.

"And he shall sit as a refiner and purifier of silver…" (Malachi 3:3)

PK knows he will be okay. He can shine his pennies with courage.

"I can do all things through Christ which strengtheneth me." (Philippians 4:13)

Supporting a child or family with disabilities can be a very challenging adventure. It can take patience, perseverance, hard work, faith and a lot of heart!

This story is based on an actual conversation.

May it bring you and those you love, hope and encouragement: most of all, the knowledge that you are never alone. Others can relate and offer support. EVERYONE has "shiny" and "less-shiny" pennies. There is also help from a loving God to help us ALL "shine those pennies"!

"For with God nothing shall be impossible." (Luke 1:37)

Made in the USA
Coppell, TX
07 April 2023

15354134R00024